WITHDRAWN

Team Spirit®

THE ORLANDO MAGIC

BY

MARK STEWART

Content Consultant
Matt Zeysing
Historian and Archivist
The Naismith Memorial Basketball Hall of Fame

NORWOODHOUSE PRESS
CHICAGO, ILLINOIS

Norwood House Press
P.O. Box 316598
Chicago, Illinois 60631

For information regarding Norwood House Press, please visit our website at:
www.norwoodhousepress.com or call 866-565-2900.

All photos courtesy of Getty Images except the following:
Associated Press (17, 23, 28, 37, 38, 40), Icon SMI (15),
Topps, Inc. (6, 9, 29, 34 both, 35 right, 40 top & bottom left, 41 right, 43),
SportsChrome (7, 20, 21, 22, 31, 36), Panini USA (14, 27),
Sports Media, Inc. (16), Matt Richman (48).
Cover Photo: Bill Baptist/Getty Images
Special thanks to Topps, Inc. and Rob Tringali

Editor: Mike Kennedy
Designer: Ron Jaffe
Project Management: Black Book Partners, LLC.
Research: Joshua Zaffos
Special thanks to William Revard, Janice Buczkowski, Clint Buczkowski,
Laura Sanborne, and Julian Santos

LIBRARY OF CONGRESS CATALOGING-IN-PUBLICATION DATA

Stewart, Mark, 1960-
  The Orlando Magic / by Mark Stewart ; content consultant, Matt Zeysing.
    p. cm. -- (Team spirit)
  Includes bibliographical references and index.
  Summary: "Presents the history and accomplishments of the Orlando Magic
basketball team. Includes highlights of players, coaches, and awards,
quotes, timeline, maps, glossary and websites"--Provided by publisher.
  ISBN-13: 978-1-59953-326-1 (library edition : alk. paper)
  ISBN-10: 1-59953-326-X (library edition : alk. paper) 1. Orlando Magic
(Basketball team)--History--Juvenile literature. 2.
Basketball--Florida--Orlando--History--Juvenile literature. I. Zeysing,
Matt. II. Title.
  GV885.52.O75S74 2009
  796.323'640975924--dc22

                                                        2009012715

Manufactured in the United States of America.

COVER PHOTO: The Magic get psyched up before a 2008–09 game.

Table of Contents

SPORTS WORDS & VOCABULARY WORDS: In this book, you will find many words that are new to you. You may also see familiar words used in new ways. The glossary on page 46 gives the meanings of basketball words, as well as "everyday" words that have special basketball meanings. These words appear in **bold type** throughout the book. The glossary on page 47 gives the meanings of vocabulary words that are not related to basketball. They appear in ***bold italic type*** throughout the book.

BASKETBALL SEASONS: Because each basketball season begins late in one year and ends early in the next, seasons are not named after years. Instead, they are written out as two years separated by a dash, for example 1944–45 or 2005–06.

Meet the Magic

In old-time movies, the good guys always wore white. In Orlando, the good guys wear white, too—with a dash of blue, a bit of black, and those impossible-to-miss *pinstripes*. The Orlando Magic make basketball fun for their fans. They launch long **3-point shots**, rattle the rim with explosive dunks, and dive on the floor for **loose balls**. It is hard to watch the Magic play without smiling.

Over the years, the Magic have given Orlando fans plenty to be happy about. The team has produced scoring champions, rebounding monsters, and record-setters at every position. The Magic even treated their fans to two exciting championship runs.

This book tells the story of the Magic. They play joyous, upbeat basketball through good times and bad. They give everything they've got no matter what the score is. And win or lose, they hold their heads high when they walk off the court. If you ever want to see the magic of basketball, buy a ticket to a game in Orlando.

Jameer Nelson watches as Rashard Lewis, Mickael Pietrus, and Dwight Howard leap high for a rebound during a 2008–09 game.

Way Back When

The 1980s were a good *decade* for **professional** basketball. The sport became more and more popular with each passing year. A banker named Jim Hewitt believed that Orlando, Florida would be the perfect place for a **National Basketball Association (NBA)** team. The area was already home to many theme parks, including Disney World. Hewitt and Pat Williams—a popular NBA *executive*—convinced the league to start a new team in Orlando. The Magic began play in the 1989–90 season.

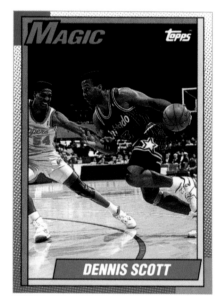

DENNIS SCOTT

Orlando struggled in its early years. But the team found some excellent players to build around, including Nick Anderson and Dennis Scott. Anderson could score from anywhere on the court. Scott was a terrific 3-point shooter.

Injuries to these two stars led the Magic to the worst record in the **Eastern Conference** in 1991–92. On the bright side, Orlando was able to get Shaquille O'Neal. The powerful young center quickly turned the team around. "Shaq" was named **Rookie of the Year** in 1992–93 and was second in the league in scoring and rebounding in 1993–94. That season the Magic made a deal for a talented guard named

Anfernee "Penny" Hardaway. He was the perfect addition to the team. Hardaway was a great shooter and passer. Orlando was hard to beat when Penny and Shaq were at their best.

In 1994–95, the Magic signed **veteran** Horace Grant. He had won three championships with the Chicago Bulls. Grant gave the young Magic an *experienced* leader. That season, Orlando raced through the **playoffs** and made it all the way to the **NBA Finals**.

LEFT: A trading card of Dennis Scott.   **ABOVE**: Nick Anderson and Shaquille O'Neal, two of Orlando's leaders during the 1990s.

Magic fans believed the team was building an NBA *dynasty*. But their dreams were dashed when Shaq left the club to play for the Los Angeles Lakers. The Magic relied on Hardaway, but without a second superstar, the team was no longer a championship *contender*. When injuries began to slow down Hardaway, it was time to rebuild the team.

GRANT HILL
MAGIC **FORWARD**

The Magic went after the top talent in the league. They added **All-Star** Grant Hill and young superstar Tracy McGrady in 2000–01. Hill was an **all-around** talent. McGrady was an explosive scorer who had not yet fulfilled his *potential*. Fans hoped this dynamic duo would lead Orlando back to the NBA Finals.

Sadly, Hill missed more than 250 games over the next six seasons. Year after year, the Magic waited for Hill to get healthy, but injuries forced him out of the **lineup**. On the other hand, McGrady blossomed into one of the league's top players. He led the NBA in scoring two years in a row. With **role players** such as Darrell Armstrong, Mike Miller, and Pat Garrity, the Magic became a competitive team. Still, they were not strong enough to challenge for a championship. That would be left to the next group of Magic stars.

LEFT: Tracy McGrady soars for a dunk. He was the NBA's scoring champion twice with the Magic.   **ABOVE**: Grant Hill, whose career with the team was slowed by injuries.

The Team Today

S ometimes for a team to reach the top, it has to hit rock-bottom first. For the Magic, that moment came early in the 2003–04 season. They lost 19 games in a row and then changed coaches. The following spring, the Magic began a rebuilding process. They used the top pick in the **draft** on a teenage center named Dwight Howard. He would become one of the NBA's true superstars.

The Magic continued to add good players. By the end of 2005–06, they were one of the league's hottest teams. In 2007–08, Rashard Lewis joined the Magic, and Jameer Nelson and Hedo Turkoglu received more playing time. The result was a division championship—Orlando's first in more than 10 years!

In 2008–09, the Magic took another step forward. They overcame bad luck and injuries to win the **Eastern Conference Finals**. For just the second time in their history, the Magic played in the NBA Finals. As the team prepared for the future, Orlando fans were eager for the city to claim its first league title.

Dwight Howard is congratulated by teammates during the 2009 NBA Finals.

Home Court

The Magic have called the same building home since they joined the NBA in 1989. It has gone by different names, including the Orlando Arena. Most fans just call it the "O-rena."

The Magic's arena is part of a sports and entertainment **complex** in downtown Orlando. It has also been used by indoor soccer and football teams. The O-rena is a popular place for concerts because of its great sound system.

In 2006, the city announced plans to build a larger arena for the Magic, to be completed before the 2010–11 season. The O-rena is one of the NBA's smallest arenas. The new building is designed to hold many more fans.

BY THE NUMBERS

- *The Magic's arena has 17,519 seats for basketball.*
- *In 2008, more than 50,000 people attended a speech by presidential candidate Barack Obama in front of the O-rena.*
- *The Magic's first win in the O-rena came on November 6, 1989. They beat the New York Knicks, 118–110.*

Hedo Turkoglu floats to the rim for a basket during a 2008–09 game in the O-rena.

Dressed for Success

The Magic's main team color has always been a shade of blue that reminds some people of the sky. During their early years, black was also an important color. The team still uses it today, but not as **prominently**.

One uniform feature that set the Magic apart was their pinstripes, which the team wore during the 1990s. Orlando's uniforms were very easy to recognize—and among the most popular in the league.

The Magic made a major change for their 10th anniversary. The team hired a famous fashion designer to give the uniforms a new look. The pinstripes disappeared, and black became less important. A few years later, the Magic started using block lettering on their uniforms. For the team's 20th season, the pinstripes returned.

The Magic's **logo** has always included a blue basketball and silver stars. The *A* in *MAGIC* is formed by a star; so is the *A* in *ORLANDO*. The shade of blue the team uses in its logo and uniforms has become lighter over the years.

ORLANDO MAGIC
SCOTT SKILES

Scott Skiles models the team's pinstriped uniform from the 1990s.

14

UNIFORM BASICS

The basketball uniform is very simple. It consists of a roomy top and baggy shorts.

- The top hangs from the shoulders, with big "scoops" for the arms and neck. This style has not changed much over the years.

- Shorts, however, have changed a lot. They used to be very short, so players could move their legs freely. In the last 20 years, shorts have gotten longer and much baggier.

Basketball uniforms look the same as they did long ago … until you look very closely. In the old days, the shorts had belts and buckles. The tops were made of a thick cotton called "jersey," which got very heavy when players sweated. Later, uniforms were made of shiny **satin**. They may have looked great, but they did not "breathe." As a result, players got very hot! Today, most uniforms are made of **synthetic** materials that soak up sweat and keep the body cool.

Rafer Alston wears the Magic's 2008–09 home uniform.

We Won!

Every team in the NBA wants to play for the championship. The Magic reached that goal in 1994–95, after only six seasons in the league. Brian Hill coached a young and energetic squad to 57 wins and first place in the **Atlantic Division**.

Center Shaquille O'Neal was unstoppable. He led the NBA with 2,315 points and averaged 29.3 points per game. Anfernee Hardaway

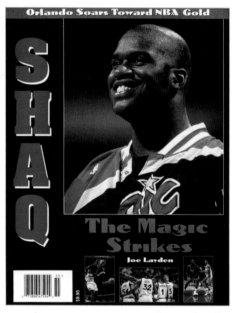

sliced through opponents for easy baskets and scored more than 20 points a game. Dennis Scott, Nick Anderson, and Brian Shaw were sharpshooters from the outside. Forward Horace Grant provided toughness and leadership.

The Magic defeated the Boston Celtics in the opening round of the playoffs. Next up were Michael Jordan and the Chicago Bulls. The Magic won twice on Chicago's home court and took the series in six games. All that stood between Orlando and a trip to the NBA Finals were the Indiana Pacers. The two teams were evenly matched. Both had great shooters, rebounders, and

LEFT: A book that celebrates Orlando's great 1994–95 season.
RIGHT: Horace Grant slams home two points in Game 7 against the Indiana Pacers.

defensive players. The Pacers were difficult to beat on their home floor, but the Magic had already proven to be "road warriors."

Orlando won the first two games at home, but the Pacers took three of the next four. That set up Game 7 in Indiana. The contest was close for two quarters. Then the Magic took over. They outscored Indiana in the second half by 14 points. Hardaway, Scott, and Anderson made one shot after another from the outside. O'Neal and Grant ruled the backboards. The final score was 105–81. When the final buzzer sounded, the Orlando players hugged one another, and streamers floated from the ceiling onto the court.

Orlando fans believed the Magic could beat anyone. They did not count on meeting the red-hot Houston Rockets in the NBA Finals. The Magic lost an **overtime** battle in Game 1. They never recovered and were swept in four games.

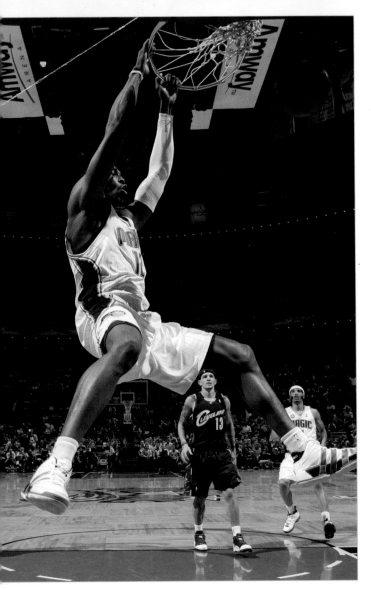

The Magic returned to the NBA Finals 24 years later. Once again, they depended on a powerful, young center. Dwight Howard played like a hurricane. He blocked shots, stole passes, tore rebounds out of the air, and made the rim shake with his monster dunks.

Howard was surrounded by talented teammates, including Hedo Turkoglu, Rashard Lewis, Mickael Pietrus, Courtney Lee, and J.J. Redick. When guard Jameer Nelson hurt his shoulder, the Magic traded for Rafer Alston. They hardly skipped a beat. Orlando finished with 59 victories, two more than the 1995 team.

When the playoffs began, the experts thought either the Boston Celtics or Cleveland Cavaliers would advance to the NBA Finals from the East. No one picked the Magic—especially after they almost lost in the opening round to the Philadelphia 76ers.

In the next round, the Magic found themselves losing to the Celtics after five games. Orlando surprised everyone by winning the last two games of the series, including Game 7 in Boston. It was on to meet LeBron James and the Cavaliers in the Eastern Conference Finals.

Cleveland had an excellent team, but the Magic were quicker at several positions. Coach Stan Van Gundy sketched out special plays to take advantage of his team's speed. The mighty Cavaliers looked helpless at times. Orlando took the series in six games. In Game 6, Howard scored 40 points, and the Magic won 103–90.

Unfortunately, the team's amazing run ended in the NBA Finals. As in 1995, Orlando faced a more experienced team. The Magic played hard, but the Los Angeles Lakers were ready for them. Orlando lost in five games. Magic fans were still proud of their team's great season.

LEFT: Dwight Howard throws down a dunk against the Cleveland Cavaliers during the 2009 playoffs.   **ABOVE**: Rashard Lewis and Hedo Turkoglu hug after Orlando's victory in the Eastern Conference Finals.

Go-To Guys

To be a true star in the NBA, you need more than a great shot. You have to be a "go-to guy"—someone teammates trust to make the winning play when the seconds are ticking away in a big game. Fans of the Magic have had a lot to cheer about over the years, including these great stars …

THE PIONEERS

NICK ANDERSON   6´ 6˝ Guard/Forward

- BORN: 1/20/1968
- PLAYED FOR TEAM: 1989–90 TO 1998–99

Nick Anderson was the first draft pick in team history. He was a threat to score anytime he had the ball. Anderson averaged double-figures in points every year he wore an Orlando uniform.

SCOTT SKILES   6´ 1˝ Guard

- BORN: 3/5/1964
- PLAYED FOR TEAM: 1989–90 TO 1993–94

No one played harder—or smarter—than Scott Skiles. He always found the open man, and he was a great team player. Skiles taught rookie Anfernee Hardaway how to play point guard in the NBA—even though he knew that Penny would one day replace him.

DENNIS SCOTT · 6′ 8″ Forward

- BORN: 9/5/1968 • PLAYED FOR TEAM: 1990–91 TO 1996–97

Dennis Scott was nicknamed "3-D" because of his accurate 3-point shot. In 1995–96, he set an NBA record with 267 baskets from beyond the arc. He also made eleven 3-pointers in a game that year.

SHAQUILLE O'NEAL · 7′ 1″ Center

- BORN: 3/6/1972 • PLAYED FOR TEAM: 1992–93 TO 1995–96

Shaquille O'Neal was the most feared player in the NBA during his time in Orlando. Shaq simply overpowered opponents with his bulk and strength. He was among the league leaders in blocks and rebounds as a rookie.

ANFERNEE HARDAWAY · · · · · · · · · · · · · · 6′ 7″ Guard

- BORN: 7/18/1971
- PLAYED FOR TEAM: 1993–94 TO 1998–99

Anfernee Hardaway could do it all. He was an excellent point guard, an accurate shooter, and a fearless attacker on offense and defense. Orlando had a winning record every year but one that Penny played for the team.

HORACE GRANT · 6′ 10″ Forward

- BORN: 7/4/1965
- PLAYED FOR TEAM: 1994–95 TO 1998–99 & 2001–02 TO 2002–03

Horace Grant joined the Magic after winning three titles with the Chicago Bulls. He brought championship experience to Orlando, plus great defense and rebounding. The Magic went to the NBA Finals in his first season with the team.

LEFT: Nick Anderson   **RIGHT**: Horace Grant

MODERN STARS

DARRELL ARMSTRONG   6′ 1″   Guard

- BORN: 6/22/1968
- PLAYED FOR TEAM: 1994–95 TO 2002–03

No one could fire up the Magic like Darrell Armstrong. He played with great emotion and *intensity*. Armstrong was a good passer and defender. His specialty was drawing **offensive fouls**.

TRACY McGRADY   6′ 8″   Forward

- BORN: 5/24/1979
- PLAYED FOR TEAM: 2000–01 TO 2003–04

The Magic hoped Tracy McGrady would team with Grant Hill to give them a great one-two punch. But "T-Mac" had to carry the load by himself when injuries slowed Hill. McGrady won the NBA scoring title twice and set a team record with 62 points in a game.

HEDO TURKOGLU   6′ 10″   Forward

- BORN: 3/19/1979   • FIRST SEASON WITH TEAM: 2004–05

The Magic signed Turkish star Hedo Turkoglu because they needed a player who could do a little of everything. Turkoglu played every position but center for Orlando. He became one of the best shooters, passers, and rebounders of any forward in the NBA.

ABOVE: Darrell Armstrong   **RIGHT**: Dwight Howard

DWIGHT HOWARD 6´ 11˝ Center

- Born: 12/8/1985 • First Season with Team: 2004–05

The Magic drafted Dwight Howard out of high school and waited for him to become a star. He surprised the team by averaging double-figures in rebounds and points in his very first season. Howard was an All-Star in his third season and was named First Team **All-NBA** a year later.

JAMEER NELSON 6´ 0˝ Guard

- Born: 2/9/1982 • First Season with Team: 2004–05

Jameer Nelson earned the job as the Magic's starting point guard in his rookie season. He improved each year and gave the team good leadership. In 2008–09, Nelson was selected to play in the All-Star Game.

RASHARD LEWIS 6´ 10˝ Forward

- Born: 8/8/1979 • First Season with Team: 2007–08

Rashard Lewis was one of the best all-around players in the league when he signed with the Magic. He proved his value by playing a new position—**power forward**—and becoming one of the NBA's best 3-point shooters.

On the Sidelines

A team that blends unusual talent the way the Magic does needs a good coach to make the club play its best. Orlando has had some excellent leaders roam the sidelines over the years. Their first was Matt Guokas. He came from a winning family *tradition*. Both he and his dad had won NBA Championships as players.

The team's second coach was Brian Hill. He led the Magic to the NBA Finals in his second season. The next year, he coached the club to 60 victories. Hill left the team in the late 1990s but returned in 2005. He became Orlando's coach again that year.

The Magic have had many other talented coaches over the years. Among the best were Doc Rivers, Chuck Daly, and Stan Van Gundy. Rivers was named NBA Coach of the Year in 1999–00. Daly is in the **Basketball Hall of Fame**. Van Gundy, who joined the team for the 2007–08 season, led the Magic to their first **Southeast Division** title that year. He was known throughout the league as a hard worker who was passionate about winning. Van Gundy guided Orlando to the NBA Finals in only his second season.

Stan Van Gundy gives his team a pep talk during the 2008–09 playoffs.

One Great Day

To win in the NBA, players must get the job done at both ends of the court. Like most new teams, the Magic struggled during their early years to balance their **roster**. Orlando, however, shot the basketball very well. Coach Matt Guokas encouraged point guard Scott Skiles to get the ball into the hands of his talented teammates. The Magic had three excellent "finishers"— Jerry Reynolds, Nick Anderson, and Dennis Scott. When they received a good pass, they knew how to put the ball in the basket.

Early in the Magic's second season, they faced the hot-shooting Denver Nuggets in Orlando. The noisy sellout crowd was expecting a high-scoring game. The Magic did not disappoint them.

26

Skiles attacked the Denver defense every time down the court. When the Magic shot, they couldn't miss. Through the first two quarters, Skiles had already done a good night's work. He had 14 **assists**.

At halftime, the Magic led 72–49. That set a team mark for points in a half. The record would last exactly 24 minutes. Skiles continued tearing up and down the floor and finding open teammates. The Magic scored 83 points in the second half to win 155–116.

ORLANDO MAGIC
JERRY REYNOLDS

Skiles broke his own team record of 18 assists in the third quarter. When the fourth quarter started, he had 25. Skiles knew he was getting close to the NBA record of 29 assists. Midway through the final period, he threw an alley-oop pass to Reynolds, who caught the ball in midair and slammed it through the basket. The crowd cheered when it was announced that Skiles had tied the NBA mark for assists.

Skiles fed Reynolds the ball three more times for easy shots, but he missed them all. The crowd went crazy each time. Skiles's 30th assist did not come until the game's final minute. Skiles spotted Reynolds open 20 feet from the basket. He passed the ball, and Reynolds made the shot. Skiles was the NBA's new assist champion.

LEFT: Matt Guokas and Scott Skiles   **ABOVE**: Jerry Reynolds

Legend Has It

Who were the best actors on the Magic?

LEGEND HAS IT that Shaquille O'Neal and Anfernee Hardaway were. This dynamic duo starred as teammates in the 1994 movie *Blue Chips*. Shaq played a character named Neon and Hardaway played a character named Butch. The movie also featured basketball legends Bob Cousy and Larry Bird. During his years with the Magic, O'Neal also starred in two other movies, *Kazaam* and *Steel*.

ABOVE: Shaquille O'Neal on the set of *Steel*.
RIGHT: Dwight Howard

Who was the best young rebounder in NBA history?

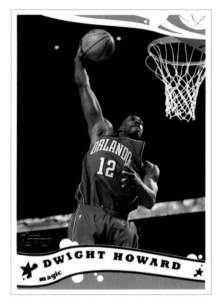

LEGEND HAS IT that Dwight Howard was. And the record book proves it! Howard was the youngest player in history to grab 20 rebounds in a game, and the youngest player to average more than 10 points and 10 rebounds in a season. Howard was also the youngest to reach 3,000, 4,000, and then 5,000 rebounds—and at 22, he was the youngest to lead the NBA in rebounding.

Who was the best player the Magic ever traded away?

LEGEND HAS IT that Chris Webber was. The Magic took Webber with the first pick in the 1993 draft. He walked to the *podium*, put on an Orlando hat, and smiled for the cameras. Fifteen minutes later, the Magic traded Webber to the Golden State Warriors, and he went on to become a superstar. Orlando also did pretty well in the deal. The Magic acquired the rights to Anfernee Hardaway, plus three first-round picks. In his second season, Hardaway led Orlando to the NBA Finals. A few years later, the team used one of the three picks to get high-scoring Mike Miller.

It Really Happened

Dennis Scott was one of the best pure shooters in basketball history. The NBA's 3-point rule seemed as if it was created for him. In 1995–96, Scott made a 3-pointer in 75 games in a row. He also set a league record with 267 baskets from behind the 3-point line.

The record Scott really wanted was the one for most 3-pointers in a game. It belonged to teammate Brian Shaw, who had once made 10 in a contest.

Late in the season, the Magic met the Atlanta Hawks in Orlando. Scott was on fire. He made seven 3-pointers in the first half. Would this be the night? The Hawks trailed at halftime but threatened to catch up early in the third quarter. Scott held them off with two more 3-pointers.

The fourth quarter was less than three minutes old when Scott swished his 10th shot from beyond the arc. With five minutes left, Scott hit number 11. Shaw gave him a big hug. He had assisted on Scott's record-tying and record-breaking shots.

Moments later, Scott left the game to a standing *ovation*. The Magic went on to win 119–104. Scott's record lasted until 2003,

Dennis Scott rises for a shot. He was deadly from behind the 3-point line, especially during the 1995–96 season.

when Kobe Bryant made a dozen 3-pointers in a game. It took 10 years before Scott's record for 3-pointers in a season was broken. Ray Allen made 269 in 2005–06.

Team Spirit

When fans fill the Magic's arena, there are few places in the NBA that are noisier. They stand up and cheer for great shots, great passes, and great defensive plays. They also cheer for the Orlando Magic Dancers. The talented members of this squad have gone on to appear in movies, commercials, and music videos.

The Magic have another group of entertainers called the Dunking Dancers. They were the first dance team to perform acrobatic slam dunks. After amazing the crowd at the 2006 All-Star Game, the Dunking Dancers were asked to perform all over the country.

Orlando's favorite court entertainer is Stuff the Magic *Mascot*. Stuff is a big green dragon that will try almost anything to amuse the fans. In the 2008–09 season, he went too far and broke his right foot doing a stunt during a game. It's not every team that can say its mascot was on **injured reserve**!

The Magic kept kids in mind while planning their new arena. It is designed to include a climbing gym, a video arcade, and plenty of basketball hoops. For families, there will be a restaurant with delicious food and an outdoor terrace.

Stuff watches as a member of the Dunking Dancers slams a ball through the hoop.

33

Timeline

The basketball season is played from October through June. That means each season takes place at the end of one year and the beginning of the next. In this timeline, the accomplishments of the Magic are shown by season.

1989–90
The Magic join the NBA.

1995–96
Orlando sets a team record with 60 victories.

1992–93
Nick Anderson scores 50 points in a game.

1994–95
The Magic reach the NBA Finals.

1996–97
Anfernee Hardaway leads the team in scoring and assists.

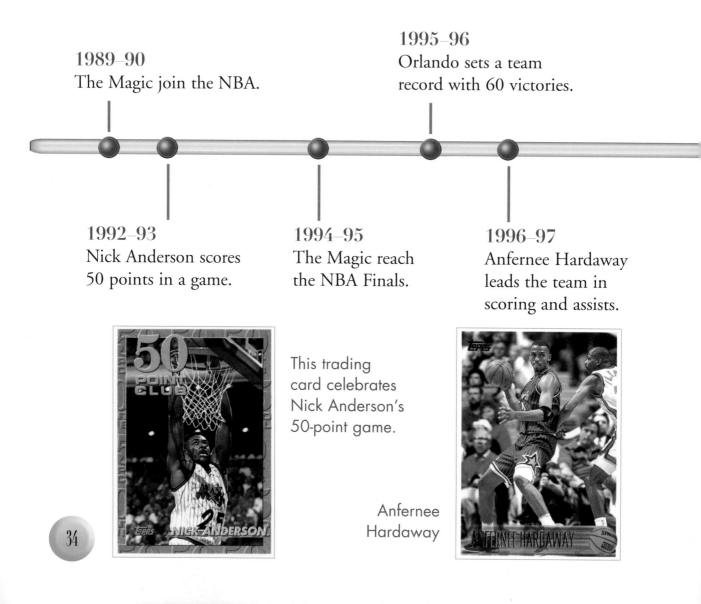

This trading card celebrates Nick Anderson's 50-point game.

Anfernee Hardaway

Tracy McGrady waves to the crowd after his 62-point performance.

Dwight Howard

2003–04
Tracy McGrady scores 62 points against the Washington Wizards.

2008–09
The Magic reach the NBA Finals for the second time.

1999–00
Doc Rivers is named NBA Coach of the Year.

2001–02
Darrell Armstrong and Troy Hudson are among the NBA's top 10 free-throw shooters.

2007–08
Dwight Howard is the NBA Slam Dunk champion.

Doc Rivers and Grant Hill

Fun Facts

LOOK, UP IN THE SKY!

In the 2008 NBA Slam Dunk Contest, Dwight Howard made his winning dunk while wearing a Superman cape. He flew through the air, caught a pass from teammate Jameer Nelson, and then dunked

the ball with his cape flapping behind him. Nearly 80 percent of the fans texting their votes picked Howard's "Superman Dunk" as the best.

THREE FOR THE MONEY

In 2008–09, the Magic set a record for 3-pointers in a game with 23 in a victory against the Sacramento Kings. At one point, the Kings had six players on the court by mistake. It still didn't help!

UNBEATABLE

From March of 1995 to March of 1996, the Magic won 40 games in a row at home.

DOUBLE-J

Jonathan Clay "J.J." Redick got his nickname from his twin sisters. Everyone knew him as "J" as a boy, but together the girls called him "J-J." Redick's middle name was his father's idea. Ken Redick is a famous potter.

NAME THAT TEAM

The Magic got their name from a fan contest held in 1986. Two names that also got a lot of votes were *Juice* and *Tropics*.

MAGIC NUMBER

The Magic have not retired the numbers of any former players. However, the team did retire number 6. That stands for the fans—the "sixth man" that helps the team win.

HOT SHOTS

In Game 3 of the 2009 NBA Finals, the Magic took 64 shots and made 40 of them. Their **shooting percentage** of 62.5 percent set a record for the NBA Finals.

LEFT: Anfernee Hardaway, who helped the Magic win 40 home games in a row.   **ABOVE**: J.J. Redick, whose real name is Jonathan Clay.

Talking Hoops

"I want to be one of the best players in the league before I finish playing. I've got the talent and the heart and the right mindset to accomplish that goal. I know I can do it."

—Dwight Howard, on his desire to be one of basketball's all-time greats

"I belong in the NBA, and the Magic needed me. That's why they took me, and I'm excited about that."

—Jameer Nelson, on why he was happy to be drafted by Orlando

"The playoffs aren't about looking good … the playoffs are about doing whatever it takes."

—Anfernee Hardaway, on winning in the playoffs

"As a point guard, I thrived in a leadership role. It was my job to make things happen on the court."

—Scott Skiles, on the responsibility of being a point guard

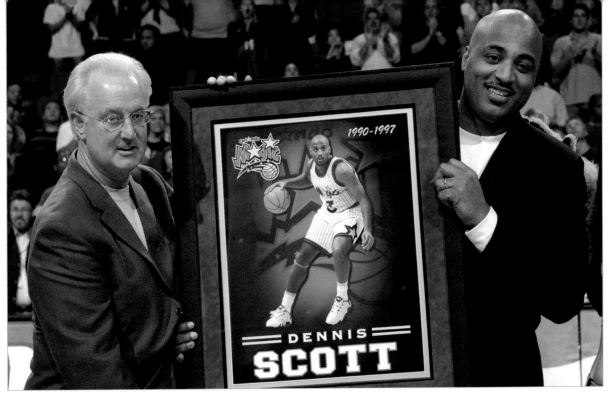

"We were so bad ... the cheerleaders stayed home and phoned in the cheers."

— *Pat Williams, joking about the Magic's early years*

"My [3-pointers] are like one of Shaq's monster dunks. It really gets the crowd and the team into the game."

— *Dennis Scott, on the value of long-distance shooting*

"People don't realize the amount of stress you put on your body— both physically and mentally—from just the wear and tear of a season."

— *Grant Hill, on why he found it hard to stay injury-free with the Magic*

LEFT: Jameer Nelson   **ABOVE**: Pat Williams and Dennis Scott

For the Record

The great Magic teams and players have left their marks on the record books. These are the "best of the best" …

Shaquille O'Neal

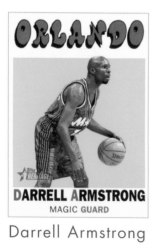

Darrell Armstrong

MAGIC AWARD WINNERS

WINNER	AWARD	SEASON
Scott Skiles	Most Improved Player	1990–91
Shaquille O'Neal	Rookie of the Year	1992–93
Darrell Armstrong	Most Improved Player	1998–99
Darrell Armstrong	Sixth Man of the Year	1998–99
Doc Rivers	Coach of the Year	1999–00
Tracy McGrady	Most Improved Player	2000–01
Mike Miller	Rookie of the Year	2000–01
Dwight Howard	NBA Slam Dunk Champion	2007–08
Hedo Turkoglu	Most Improved Player	2007–08
Dwight Howard	NBA Defensive Player of the Year	2008–09

Dwight Howard does his winning "Superman Dunk" during the 2008 Slam Dunk Contest.

MAGIC ACHIEVEMENTS

ACHIEVEMENT	SEASON
Atlantic Division Champions	1994–95
Eastern Conference Champions	1994–95
Atlantic Division Champions	1995–96
Southeast Division Champions	2007–08
Southeast Division Champions	2008–09
Eastern Conference Champions	2008–09

NBA ALL-STARS
★ 2000-01/ EAST TEAM ★

HERITAGE

TRACY
McGRADY

GUARD-
FORWARD

MAGIC

ABOVE: Tracy McGrady, the NBA's Most Improved Player for the 2000–01 season.
LEFT: Mike Miller, the NBA's Rookie of the Year for the 2000–01 season.

Pinpoints

T he history of a basketball team is made up of many smaller stories. These stories take place all over the map—not just in the city a team calls "home." Match the pushpins on these maps to the Team Facts and you will begin to see the story of the Magic unfold!

TEAM FACTS

1   Orlando, Florida—*The Magic have played here since 1989–90.*

2   Atlanta, Georgia—*Dwight Howard was born here.*

3   Gastonia, North Carolina—*Darrell Armstrong was born here.*

4   Hagerstown, Maryland—*Dennis Scott was born here.*

5   Newark, New Jersey—*Shaquille O'Neal was born here.*

6   Chester, Pennsylvania—*Jameer Nelson was born here.*

7   Chicago, Illinois—*Nick Anderson was born here.*

8   Memphis, Tennessee—*Anfernee Hardaway was born here.*

9   Pineville, Louisiana—*Rashard Lewis was born here.*

10   Dallas, Texas—*Grant Hill was born here.*

11   Indio, California—*Stan Van Gundy was born here.*

12   Istanbul, Turkey—*Hedo Turkoglu was born here.*

Dwight Howard

Play Ball

Basketball is a sport played by two teams of five players. NBA games have four 12-minute quarters—48 minutes in all—and the team that scores the most points when time has run out is the winner. Most baskets count for two points. Players who make shots from beyond the three-point line receive an extra point. Baskets made from the free-throw line count for one point. Free throws are penalty shots awarded to a team, usually after an opponent has committed a foul. A foul is called when one player makes hard contact with another.

Players can move around all they want, but the player with the ball cannot. He must bounce the ball with one hand or the other (but never both) in order to go from one part of the court to another. As long as he keeps "dribbling," he can keep moving.

In the NBA, teams must attempt a shot every 24 seconds, so there is little time to waste. The job of the defense is to make it as difficult as possible for the offense to take a good shot—and to grab the ball if the other team shoots and misses.

This may sound simple, but anyone who has played the game knows that basketball can be very complicated. Every player on the court has a job to do. Different players have different strengths and weaknesses. The coach must mix these players in just the right way and teach them to work together as one.

The more you play and watch basketball, the more "little things" you are likely to notice. The next time you watch a game, look for these plays:

PLAY LIST

ALLEY-OOP—A play in which the passer throws the ball just to the side of the rim—so a teammate can catch it and dunk in one motion.

BACK-DOOR PLAY—A play in which the passer waits for a teammate to fake the defender away from the basket—then throws him the ball when he cuts back toward the basket.

KICK-OUT—A play in which the ball handler waits for the defense to surround him—then quickly passes to a teammate who is open for an outside shot. The ball is not really kicked in this play; the term comes from the action of pinball machines.

NO-LOOK PASS—A play in which a passer fools the defense by looking in one direction, then making a surprise pass to a teammate.

PICK-AND-ROLL—A play in which one player blocks, or "picks off," a teammate's defender with his body, then in the confusion cuts to the basket for a pass.

Glossary

BASKETBALL WORDS TO KNOW

3-POINT SHOTS—Baskets made from behind the 3-point line.

ALL-AROUND—Good at all parts of the game.

ALL-NBA—An honor given at the end of the season to the NBA's best players at each position.

ALL-STAR—A player selected to play in the annual All-Star Game.

ASSISTS—Passes that lead to successful shots.

ATLANTIC DIVISION—A group of teams that play in a region that is close to the Atlantic Ocean.

BASKETBALL HALL OF FAME—The museum in Springfield, Massachusetts where the game's greatest players are honored; these players are often called "Hall of Famers."

DRAFT—The annual meeting during which NBA teams choose from a group of the best college players. The draft is held each summer.

EASTERN CONFERENCE—A group of teams that play in the East. The winner of the Eastern Conference meets the winner of the Western Conference in the league finals.

EASTERN CONFERENCE FINALS—The playoff series that determines which team from the East will play the best team from the West for the NBA Championship.

INJURED RESERVE—An official listing of players who are unable to play because of an injury.

LINEUP—The list of players who are playing in a game.

LOOSE BALLS—Balls that are not controlled by either team.

NATIONAL BASKETBALL ASSOCIATION (NBA)—The professional league that has been operating since 1946–47.

NBA FINALS—The playoff series that decides the champion of the league.

OFFENSIVE FOULS—Fouls committed by a member of the team controlling the ball.

OVERTIME—The extra period played when a game is tied after 48 minutes.

PLAYOFFS—The games played after the season to determine the league champion.

POWER FORWARD—The bigger and stronger of a team's two forwards.

PROFESSIONAL—A player or team that plays a sport for money.

ROLE PLAYERS—People who are asked to do specific things when they are in a game.

ROOKIE OF THE YEAR—The annual award given to the league's best first-year player.

ROSTER—The list of players on a team.

SHOOTING PERCENTAGE—A statistic that measures shooting accuracy by dividing shots made by shots taken.

SOUTHEAST DIVISION—A division for teams that play in the southeast part of the country.

VETERAN—A player with great experience.

OTHER WORDS TO KNOW

COMPLEX—A series of buildings grouped together.

CONTENDER—A person or team that competes for a championship.

DECADE—A period of 10 years; also specific periods, such as the 1950s.

DYNASTY—A family, group, or team that maintains power over time.

EXECUTIVE—A person who makes important decisions for a company.

EXPERIENCED—Having knowledge and skill in a job.

INTENSITY—The strength and energy of a thought or action.

LOGO—A symbol or design that represents a company or team.

MASCOT—An animal or person believed to bring a group good luck.

OVATION—A long, loud cheer.

PINSTRIPES—Thin stripes.

PODIUM—A stand used by a speaker.

POTENTIAL—The ability to become better.

PROMINENTLY—Easily noticed.

SATIN—A smooth, shiny fabric.

SYNTHETIC—Made in a laboratory, not in nature.

TRADITION—A belief or custom that is handed down from generation to generation.

Places to Go

ON THE ROAD

ORLANDO MAGIC
600 West Amelia Street
Orlando, Florida 32801
(407) 839-3900

NAISMITH MEMORIAL BASKETBALL HALL OF FAME
1000 West Columbus Avenue
Springfield, Massachusetts 01105
(877) 4HOOPLA

ON THE WEB

THE NATIONAL BASKETBALL ASSOCIATION   www.nba.com
  • *Learn more about the league's teams, players, and history*

THE ORLANDO MAGIC   www.nba.com/magic
  • *Learn more about the Magic*

THE BASKETBALL HALL OF FAME   www.hoophall.com
  • *Learn more about history's greatest players*

ON THE BOOKSHELF

To learn more about the sport of basketball, look for these books at your library or bookstore:

  • Stewart, Mark and Kennedy, Mike. *Swish: the Quest for Basketball's Perfect Shot.* Minneapolis, Minnesota: Millbrook Press, 2009.
  • Ramen, Fred. *Basketball: Rules, Tips, Strategy & Safety.* New York, New York: Rosen Central, 2007.
  • Labrecque, Ellen. *Basketball.* Ann Arbor, Michigan: Cherry Lake Publishing, 2009.
  • Wyckoff, Edwin Brit. *The Man Who Invented Basketball: James Naismith and His Amazing Game.* Berkeley Heights, New Jersey: Enslow Elementary, 2008.

47

Index

The Team

MARK STEWART has written more than 20 books on basketball, and over 100 sports books for kids. He grew up in New York City during the 1960s rooting for the Knicks and Nets, and now takes his two daughters, Mariah and Rachel, to watch them play. Mark comes from a family of writers. His grandfather was Sunday Editor of *The New York Times* and his mother was Articles Editor of *The Ladies Home Journal* and *McCall's*. Mark has profiled hundreds of athletes over the last 20 years. He has also written several books about his native New York, and New Jersey, his home today. Mark is a graduate of Duke University, with a degree in history. He lives with his daughters and wife, Sarah, overlooking Sandy Hook, New Jersey.

MATT ZEYSING is the resident historian at the Basketball Hall of Fame in Springfield, Massachusetts. His research interests include the origins of the game of basketball, the development of professional basketball in the first half of the 20th century, and the culture and meaning of basketball in American society.